A LOOK AT NATURE'S CYCLES

THE WATER CYCLE

BY SANTANA HUNT

Gareth Stevens
PUBLISHING

CRASHCOURSE

Please visit our website, www.garethstevens.com. For a free color catalog of all our high-quality books, call toll free 1-800-542-2595 or fax 1-877-542-2596.

Cataloging-in-Publication Data
Names: Hunt, Santana.
Title: The water cycle / Santana Hunt.
Description: New York : Gareth Stevens Publishing, 2020. | Series: A look at nature's cycles | Includes glossary and index.
Identifiers: ISBN 9781538241226 (pbk.) | ISBN 9781538241240 (library bound) | ISBN 9781538241233 (6 pack)
Subjects: LCSH: Hydrologic cycle--Juvenile literature. | Water--Juvenile literature.
Classification: LCC GB662.3 .H86 2020 | DDC 551.48--dc23

First Edition

Published in 2020 by
Gareth Stevens Publishing
111 East 14th Street, Suite 349
New York, NY 10003

Designer: Sarah Liddell
Editor: Kristen Nelson

Photo credits: Cover, p. 1 (main) tusharkoley/Shutterstock.com; cover, p. 1 (inset) peresanz/Shutterstock.com; arrow background used throughout Inka1/Shutterstock.com; p. 5 IgorShishkin/Shutterstock.com; p. 7 jokerpro/Shutterstock.com; p. 9 Maridav/Shutterstock.com; p. 11 MicroOne/Shutterstock.com; p. 13 vidalgo/Shutterstock.com; p. 15 detchana wangkheeree/Shutterstock.com; p. 17 Vadym Lavra/Shutterstock.com; p. 19 Justin Torres/Shutterstock.com; p. 21 NosorogUA/Shutterstock.com; p. 23 David Crockett Photo/Shutterstock.com; p. 25 mady70/Shutterstock.com; p. 27 Peter Hermes Furian/Shutterstock.com; p. 29 Lena May/Shutterstock.com; p. 30 3xy/Shutterstock.com.

Printed in the United States of America

CPSIA compliance information: Batch #CS19GS: For further information contact Gareth Stevens, New York, New York at 1-800-542-2595.

CONTENTS

Words in the glossary appear in **bold** type the first time they are used in the text.

WATER MOVES

Earth's **cycles** are amazing! Scientists often break them down into steps that make them easier to understand. One is the water cycle. It shows the movement of water in and on Earth, as well as in the **atmosphere**!

MAKE THE GRADE

Water is always moving through the water cycle!
It's been doing so for billions of years.

HOW MUCH WATER?

There are about 332.6 million cubic miles (1.38 billion cu km) of water on Earth. About 97 percent of this water is salt water found in oceans. Much of the water that is part of the water cycle comes from the oceans.

MAKE THE GRADE

There is water in the land under your feet!
This is called groundwater.

The other 3 percent of Earth's water is fresh water. More than two-thirds of this fresh water is in ice caps and **glaciers**! A very small part of Earth's fresh water is found in lakes, rivers, and other bodies of water.

MAKE THE GRADE

Much of the water on Earth is unable to be used by people, whether because it's salt water, part of the atmosphere, or deep underground.

9

A STARTING POINT

The water cycle has no real starting point. All the steps of the cycle are happening all the time! One of the major steps is evaporation. This is the change of water from its liquid form to a gas, or water vapor.

MAKE THE GRADE

About 90 percent of evaporated water in the
water cycle comes from Earth's bodies of water.

WATER'S STATES OF MATTER

GAS

LIQUID

SOLID

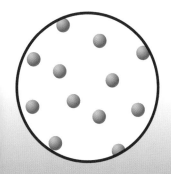

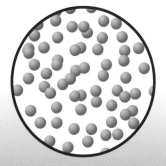

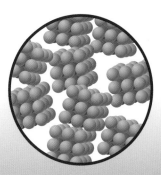

Heat energy drives evaporation. It causes the **molecules** in water to speed up. Once they're moving fast enough, they leave the water's surface, now as water vapor. Water evaporates in this way from land, too.

MAKE THE GRADE

Water moving through a plant and out its **stomata** to evaporate is called transpiration. About 10 percent of all water vapor in the water cycle comes from transpiration.

BUILDING CLOUDS

Another main step in the water cycle occurs as water vapor rises. It begins to cool and change back into a liquid. This is called condensation. The water molecules mix with dust and other **particles** in the air to form clouds.

MAKE THE GRADE

Fog is another example of condensation we can see.

BACK TO EARTH

Clouds, formed through condensation, are the main way water from the atmosphere reaches Earth's surface. This happens by precipitation, or the water let go from clouds as rain, hail, snow, or sleet. Most precipitation around the world is rain.

MAKE THE GRADE

Sometimes, snow and ice become water vapor without changing to a liquid first. This is called sublimation.

17

The water from precipitation reenters the water cycle in a few ways. Some precipitation just evaporates again and returns to the atmosphere. Much of it flows over land into bodies of water, including oceans, rivers, and lakes. This is called runoff.

MAKE THE GRADE

When water flows over trash or fields that have been **fertilized**, runoff can spread pollution.

INTO THE GROUND

The water from precipitation may **seep** into the soil. This step of the water cycle is called infiltration. Infiltration can help refill aquifers, or the rock underground that can hold water that people often use.

MAKE THE GRADE

Some aquifers are very deep and store water for thousands of years!

AQUIFER

Water that has infiltrated the ground may simply flow up and become part of a body of water. It may be absorbed, or taken in, by plants' roots. Water not used by the plant will be let out in transpiration!

MAKE THE GRADE

When an aquifer is filled with groundwater, the water may break through Earth's surface as a spring.

WATER STORES

Water stored as ice and glaciers doesn't move through the water cycle like that in surface water. It may remain frozen for a long time! However, as Earth's **climate** changes, this ice may melt and rejoin the water cycle as part of the oceans.

MAKE THE GRADE

Nearly 90 percent of Earth's ice is found in Antarctica.
The other 10 percent is part of Greenland's ice cap.

GLOBAL MOVEMENT

Currents in the ocean move a lot of water around the world. They greatly affect the water cycle since they're continuously moving warmer water to cooler areas and cooler water to warmer areas. The Kuroshio Current, near Japan, is the largest current.

MAKE THE GRADE

The Gulf Stream, shown below, is a major current that moves warm water from the Gulf of Mexico east across the Atlantic Ocean. It moves as fast as a car on a highway!

 WARM WATER   **COOL WATER**

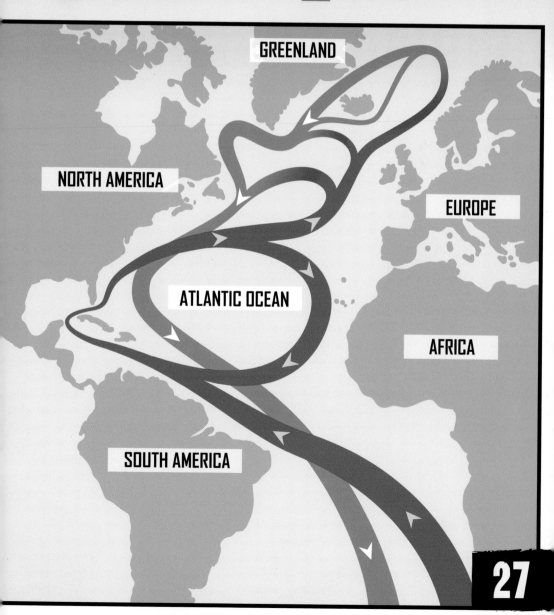

GREENLAND

NORTH AMERICA

EUROPE

ATLANTIC OCEAN

AFRICA

SOUTH AMERICA

27

It's easy to see the water cycle at work on a rainy day. But, even if you can't see it, water is moving around us all the time! On a clear day, there are water molecules too small for us to see in the air.

MAKE THE GRADE

If all the water in Earth's atmosphere rained down on us at once,
it would only be about 1 inch (2.5 cm) deep around the world!

THE
WATER CYCLE

CONDENSATION

TRANSPIRATION

PRECIPITATION

EVAPORATION

INFILTRATION

GLOSSARY

atmosphere: the mixture of gases that surround a planet

climate: the average weather conditions of a place over a period of time

current: a continuous movement of water or air in the same direction

cycle: a series of events that repeats

fertilize: to make land better able to produce plants by adding something

glacier: a very large area of ice that moves slowly down a slope or valley or over a wide area of land

molecule: a very small piece of matter

particle: a very small piece of something

seep: to pass slowly through small openings in something

stoma: a tiny hole on the underside of a plant leaf. The plural is stomata.

FOR MORE INFORMATION

BOOKS

Berne, Emma Carlson. *From River to Raindrop: The Water Cycle.* Minneapolis, MN: Lerner Publications, 2018.

Bradshaw, Aiden. *Freshwater Crisis.* New York, NY: PowerKids Press, 2018.

WEBSITES

Cycles of the Earth System
eo.ucar.edu/kids/green/cycles1.htm
Find out more about other natural cycles on Earth.

The Water Cycle!
www.natgeokids.com/uk/discover/science/nature/water-cycle/
Review the water cycle on this National Geographic website for kids.

Publisher's note to educators and parents: Our editors have carefully reviewed this website to ensure that it is suitable for students. Many websites change frequently, however, and we cannot guarantee that a site's future contents will continue to meet our high standards of quality and educational value. Be advised that students should be closely supervised whenever they access the internet.

INDEX